SCREEN GUIDE FOR AMERICANS

Screen Guide for Americans
is in the public domain.
Original work by Ayn Rand not under copyright.
Cover photo of Ayn Rand may not be copied or reproduced in any way
except for and only in representations of this book.
Foreword may not be copied or reproduced in any form, in total or in part,
without express written permission from the publisher.

Cover photo: Courtesy of **Tom Bowden**,
research fellow at the **Ayn Rand Institute**.

ISBN (Paperback): 978-1-950464-48-7
ISBN (eBook): 978-1-950464-49-4

Edition 1, 2023

Screen Guide for Americans

AYN RAND

OffBeatReads

Forword

Many years ago, when I began examining various philosophies, it didn't take long for me to notice something disturbing. Collectivists spared no energy in railing philosophers who advocated individualism. I was sad when I observed this, because I thought the prevailing attitude was one that favored individual rights. Among the loud collectivists were Marxists and Communists who remained convinced that the, "greater good" argument was the moral choice.

Having always been someone who puts great value on ideas and creating and truth, this made no sense. I questioned them. "If you believe in putting more importance on society than the individual, why are you not open to ideas that could potentially benefit those in that society?" The answers were hardly sufficient and never thought out.

It never stands the test of logic, *or any test*, why a system of government would rely on reducing the value and rights of its people. Reducing the rights of the people in the name of the greater good is the means by which power is obtained, rather than the means to achieve something better.

Watch a socialist scowl at a wealthy person, or watch a Communist fume when an individual claims a right to property. In the former, it is an automatic assumption that the wealthy took success, opportunity, or goods from the poor. In the latter, it is understood that property exists to benefit the community.

No matter what a system is titled politically, once it esteems the group over the individual and has convinced enough people of it's moral intent, it's game over. All citizens are members by default, whether they believe or not. Rights are handed over, and those in power seek more power (not equity or fairness as they claim), until horrors such as we have seen in history occur again. The potential for danger is real. It is for this reason that forms of collectivism must be acknowledged, and systems such as Communism must at least be dealt with on the same level as that at which they are being introduced.

On October 20, 1947, Ayn Rand testified as a friendly witness in front of **HUAC** (House Un-American Activities Committee). Aside from any positives or negatives resulting from the existence of this committee, the concern was real. The infiltration of dangerous ideas isn't always through grassroots efforts, chanted slogans, or honest conversation.

It is for this reason Ayn Rand wrote the pamphlet that follows for the **Motion Picture Alliance for the Preservation of American Ideals**. Rand issued a statement that is important to know, saying the pamphlet was, *"intended as a guide, and not as a forced restriction upon anyone"*. Recognizing that each individual must do his or her own thinking, the entire alliance was opposed to any mandates or industry code. Rand stated further that the guide was for the, "*independent judgment and for the voluntary action of every honest man in the motion picture industry*".

Can an astute mind of today pick up continued propaganda in movies, or elsewhere in our culture? History does indeed repeat itself, and those who seek power are relentless. Here is **Screen Guide for Americans**, with a copy of the **Statement of Principles** issued by the Motion Picture Alliance added as a bonus in the back.

Here's to doing your own thinking,
Robert Kimbrell
OffBeat Publishing

The Screen Guide for Americans

The influence of Communists in Hollywood is due, not to their own power, but to the unthinking carelessness of those who profess to oppose them. Red propaganda has been put over in some films produced by innocent men, often by loyal Americans who deplore the spread of Communism throughout the world and wonder why it is spreading.

If you wish to protect your pictures from being used for Communistic purposes, the first thing to do is to drop the delusion that political propaganda consists only of political slogans.

Politics is not a separate field in itself. Political ideas do not come out of thin air. They are the result of the **moral**

premises which men have accepted. Whatever people believe to be the good, right and proper human actions — **that** will determine their political opinions. If men believe that every independent action is vicious, they will vote for every measure to control human beings and to suppress human freedom. If men believe that the American system is unjust, they will support those who wish to destroy it.

The purpose of the Communists in Hollywood is **not** the production of political movies openly advocating Communism. Their purpose is **to corrupt our moral premises by corrupting non-political movies** — by introducing small, casual bits of propaganda into innocent stories — thus making people absorb the basic premises of Collectivism **by indirection and implication**.

Few people would take Communism straight. But a constant stream of hints, lines, touches and suggestions battering the public from the screen will act like the drops of water that split a rock if continued long enough. The rock they are trying to split is Americanism.

We present below a list of the more common devices used to turn non-political pictures into carriers of political propaganda. It is a guide list for all those who do not wish to help advance the cause of Communism.

It is intended as a guide, and not as a forced restriction upon anyone. We are unalterably opposed to any political "industry code," to any group agreement or any manner of forbidding any political opinion to anyone by any form of collective force or pressure. There can be no "group insurance" in the field of ideas. Each man has to do his own thinking. We merely offer this list to the independent judgment and for the voluntary action of every honest man in the motion picture industry.

1. Don't Take Politics Lightly.

Don't fool yourself by saying, "I'm not

interested in politics," and then pretending that politics do not exist.

We are living in an age when politics is the most burning question in everybody's mind. The whole world is torn by a great political issue — Freedom or Slavery, which means Americanism or Totalitarianism. Half the world is in ruins after a war fought over political ideas. To pretend at such a time that political ideas are not important and that people pay no attention to them, is worse than irresponsible.

It is the avowed purpose of the Communists to insert propaganda into movies. Therefore, there are only two possible courses of action open to you, if you want to keep your pictures clean of subversive propaganda:

1. If you have no time or inclination to study political ideas — then do not hire Reds to work on your pictures.
2. If you wish to employ Reds, but intend to keep their politics out of your movies — then study political ideas

and learn how to recognize propaganda when you see it.

But to hire Communists on the theory that "they won't put over any politics on me" and then remain ignorant and indifferent to the subject of politics, while the Reds are trained propaganda experts — is an attitude for which there can be no excuse.

2. Don't Smear the Free Enterprise System.

Don't pretend that Americanism and the Free Enterprise System are two things. They are inseparable, like body and soul. The basic principle of inalienable individual rights, which is Americanism, can be translated into practical reality **only** in the form of the economic system of Free Enterprise. That was the system established by the American Constitution, the system which made America the best and greatest country on earth. You may preach any other form of economics, if you wish. But if you do so, don't pretend that you are preaching Americanism.

Don't pretend that you are upholding the Free Enterprise System in some vague, general, undefined way, while preaching the specific ideas that oppose it and destroy it.

Don't attack individual rights, individual freedom, private action, private initiative, and private property. These things are essential parts of the Free Enterprise System, without which it cannot exist.

Don't preach the superiority of public ownership as such over private ownership. **Don't** preach or imply that all publicly-owned projects are noble, humanitarian undertakings by grace of the mere fact that they are publicly-owned — while preaching, at the same time, that private property or the defense of private property rights is the expression of some sort of vicious greed, of anti-social selfishness or evil.

3. Don't Smear Industrialists.

Don't spit into your own face or, worse, pay miserable little rats to do it.

You, as a motion picture producer, are an industrialist. All of us are employees of an industry which gives us a good living. There is an old fable about a pig who filled his belly with acorns, then started digging to undermine the roots of the oak from which the acorns came. Don't let's allow that pig to become our symbol.

Throughout American history, the best of American industrialists were men who embodied the highest virtues: productive genius, energy, initiative, independence, courage. Socially (if "social significance" interests you) they were among the greatest of all benefactors, because it is they who created the opportunities for achieving the unprecedented material wealth of the industrial age.

In our own day, all around us, there are countless examples of self-made men who rose from the ranks and achieved great industrial success through their energy, ability and honest productive effort.

Yet all too often industrialists, bankers, and businessmen are presented on the screen as villains, crooks, chiselers or exploiters. One such picture may be taken as non-political or accidental. A constant stream of such pictures becomes pernicious political propaganda: It creates hatred for all businessmen in the mind of the audience, and makes people receptive to the cause of Communism.

While motion pictures have a strict code that forbids us to offend or insult any group or nation — while we dare not present in an unfavorable light the tiniest Balkan kingdom — we permit ourselves to smear and slander American businessmen in the most irresponsibly dishonest manner.

It is true that there are vicious businessmen — just as there are vicious men in any other class or profession. But we have been practicing an outrageous kind of double standard: we do not attack individual representatives of any other group, class or nation, in order not to imply an attack on the whole group; yet when we present individual businessmen as monsters, we claim that no reflection on the whole class of businessmen was intended.

It's got to be one or the other. This sort of double standard can deceive nobody and can serve nobody's purpose except that of the Communists.

It is the **moral** — (no, not just political, but **moral**) — duty of every decent man in the motion picture industry to throw into the ashcan, where it belongs, every story that smears industrialists as such.

4. Don't smear Wealth.

In a free society — such as America — wealth is achieved through production, and through the voluntary exchange of one's goods or services. You cannot hold production as evil — nor can you hold as evil a man's right to keep the result of his own effort.

Only savages and Communists get rich by force — that is, by looting the property of others. It is a basic American principle that each man is free to work for his own benefit and to go as far as his ability will carry him; and his property is his — whether he has made one dollar or one million dollars.

If the villain in your story happens to be rich — **don't** permit lines of dialogue suggesting that he is the typical representative of a whole social class, the symbol of all the rich. Keep it clear in your mind **and in your script** that his villainy is due to his own personal character — not to his wealth or class.

If you do not see the difference between wealth honestly produced and wealth looted — you are preaching the ideas of Communism. You are implying that all property and all human labor should belong to the State. And you are inciting men to crime: If all wealth is evil, no matter how acquired, why should a man bother to earn it? He might as well seize it by robbery or expropriation.

It is the proper wish of every decent American to stand on his own feet, earn his own living, and be as good at it as he can — that is, get as rich as he can by honest exchange.

Stop insulting him and stop defaming his proper ambition. Stop giving him — and yourself — a guilt complex by spreading unthinkingly the slogans of Communism. **Put an end to that pernicious modern hypocrisy: everybody wants to get rich and almost everybody feels that he must apologize for it.**

5. Don't Smear the Profit Motive.

If you denounce the profit motive, what is it that you wish men to do? Work without reward, like slaves, for the benefit of the State?

An industrialist has to be interested in profit. In a free economy, he can make a profit **only** if he makes a good product which people are willing to buy. What do you want him to do? Should he sell his product at a loss? If so, how long is he to remain in business? And at whose expense?

Don't give to your characters — as a sign of villainy, as a damning characteristic — a desire to make money. Nobody wants to, or should, work without payment, and nobody does — except a slave. There is nothing dishonorable about a pursuit of money in a free economy, because money can be earned only by productive effort.

If what you mean, when you denounce it, is a desire to make money dishonestly or immorally — then say so. Make it clear that what you denounce is dishonesty, **not** money-making. Make it clear that you are denouncing evil-doers, **not** capitalists. Don't toss out careless generalities which imply that there is no difference between the two. **That** is what the Communists want you to imply.

6. Don't Smear Success.

America was made by the idea that personal achievement and personal success are each man's proper and moral goal.

There are many forms of success: spiritual, artistic, industrial, financial. All these forms, in any field of honest endeavor, are good, desirable and admirable. Treat them as such.

Don't permit any disparagement or defamation of personal success. It is the Communists' intention to make people think that personal success is somehow achieved at the expense of others and that every successful man has hurt somebody by becoming successful.

It is the Communists' aim to discourage all personal effort and to drive men into a hopeless, dispirited, gray herd of robots who have lost all personal ambition, who are easy to rule, willing to obey and willing to exist in selfless servitude to the State.

America is based on the ideal of man's dignity and self-respect. Dignity and self-respect are impossible without a sense of personal achievement. When you defame success, you defame human dignity.

America is the land of the self-made man. Say so on the screen.

7. Don't Glorify Failure.

Failure, in itself, is not admirable. And while every man meets with failure somewhere in his life, the admirable thing is his courage in **overcoming it — not** the fact that he failed.

Failure is no disgrace — but it is certainly no brand of virtue or nobility, either.

It is the Communist's intention to make men accept misery, depravity and degradation as their natural lot in life. This is done by presenting every kind of failure as sympathetic, as a sign of goodness and virtue — while every kind of success is presented as a sign of evil. This implies that only the evil can succeed under our American system — while the good are to be found in the gutter.

Don't present all the poor as good and all

the rich as evil. In judging a man's character, poverty is no disgrace — but it is no virtue, either; wealth is no virtue — but it is certainly no disgrace.

8. Don't Glorify Depravity.

Don't present sympathetic studies of depravity. Go easy on stories about murderers, perverts and all the rest of that sordid stuff. If you use such stories, **don't** place yourself and the audience on the side of the criminal, **don't** create sympathy for him, **don't** give him excuses and justifications, **don't** imply that he "couldn't help it."

If you preach that a depraved person "couldn't help it," you are destroying the basis of all morality. You are implying that men cannot be held responsible for their evil acts, because man has no power to choose between good and evil; if so, then all moral precepts are futile, and men must resign themselves to the idea that they are helpless, irresponsible animals. **Don't** help to spread such an idea.

When you pick these stories for their purely sensational value, you do not realize that you are dealing with one of the most crucial philosophical issues. These stories represent a profoundly insidious attack on all moral principles and all religious precepts. It is a basic tenet of Marxism that man has no freedom of moral or intellectual choice; that he is only a soulless, witless collection of meat and glands, open to any sort of "conditioning" by anybody. The Communists intend to become the "conditioners."

There is too much horror and depravity in the world at present. If people see nothing but horror and depravity on the screen, you will merely add to their despair by driving in the impression that nothing better is possible to men or can be expected of life, which is what the Communists want people to think. Communism thrives on despair. Men without hope are easily ruled.

Don't excuse depravity. **Don't** drool over weaklings as conditioned "victims of circumstances" (or of "background" or of "society"), who "couldn't help it." You are actually providing an excuse and an alibi for the worst instincts in the weakest members of your audience.

Don't tell people that man is a helpless, twisted, drooling, sniveling, neurotic weakling. Show the world an **American** kind of man, for a change.

9. Don't Deify "The Common Man."

"The common man" is one of the worst slogans of Communism — and too many of us have fallen for it, without thinking.

It is only in Europe — under social caste systems where men are divided into "aristocrats" and "commoners" — that one can talk about defending the "common man." What does the word "common" mean in America?

Under the American system, all men are equal before the law. Therefore, if anyone is classified as "common" — he can be called "common" only in regard to his personal qualities. It then means that he has no outstanding abilities, no outstanding virtues, no outstanding intelligence. Is **that** an object of glorification?

In the Communist doctrine, **it is**. Communism preaches the reign of mediocrity, the destruction of all individuality and all personal distinction, the turning of men into "masses," which means an undivided, undifferentiated, impersonal, average, **common** herd.

In the American doctrine, no man is **common**. Every man's personality is unique — and it is respected as such. He may have qualities which he shares with others; but his virtue is not gauged by how much he resembles others — **that** is the Communist doctrine; his virtue is gauged by his personal distinction, great or small.

In America, no man is scorned or penalized if his ability is small. But neither is he praised, extolled and glorified for the **smallness** of his ability.

America is the land of the **uncommon man**. It is the land where man is free to develop his genius — and to get its just rewards. It is the land where each man tries to develop whatever quality he might possess and to rise to whatever degree he can, great or modest. It is **not** the land where one is taught that one is small and ought to remain small. It is **not** the land where one glories or is taught to glory in one's mediocrity.

No self-respecting man in America is or thinks of himself as "little," no matter how poor he might be. **That**, precisely, is the difference between an American working man and a European serf.

Don't ever use any lines about "the common man" or "the little people." It is not the American idea to be either "common" or "little."

10. Don't Deify the Collective.

This point requires your careful and thoughtful attention.

There is a great difference between free co-operation and forced collectivism. It is the difference between the United States and Soviet Russia. But the Communists are very skillful at hiding the difference and selling you the second under the guise of the first. You might miss it. The audience won't.

Co-operation is the free association of men who work together by voluntary agreement, each deriving from it his own personal benefit.

Collectivism is the forced herding together of men into a group, with the individual having no choice about it, no personal motive, no personal reward, and subordinating himself blindly to the will of others.

Keep this distinction clearly in mind — in order to judge whether what you are asked to glorify is American co-operation or Soviet Collectivism.

Don't preach that everybody should be and act alike.

Don't fall for such drivel as "I don't wanna be dif'rent — I wanna be just like ever'body else." You've heard this one in endless variations. If ever there was an un-

American attitude, this is it. America is the country where every man wants to be **different** — and most men succeed at it.

If you preach that it is evil to be different — you teach every particular group of men to hate every other group, every minority, every person, for being different from them; thus you lay the foundation for racial hatred.

Don't preach that **all** mass action is good, and **all** individual action is evil. It is true that there are vicious individuals; it is also true that there are vicious groups. Both must be judged by their specific actions — and not treated as an issue of "the one" against "the many," with the many always right and the one always wrong.

Remember that it is the Communists' aim to preach the supremacy, the holy virtue of the group — as opposed to the individual. It is not America's aim. Nor yours.

11. Don't Smear an Independent Man.

This is part of the same issue as the preceding point.

The Communists' chief purpose is to destroy every form of independence — independent work, independent action, independent property, independent thought, an independent mind, or an independent man.

Conformity, alikeness, servility, submission and obedience are necessary to establish a Communist slave-state. **Don't** help the Communists to teach men to acquire these attitudes.

Don't fall for the old Communist trick of thinking that an independent man or an individualist is one who crushes and exploits others — such as a dictator. An independent man is one who stands alone and respects the same right of others, who does not rule nor serve, who neither sacrifices himself nor others. A dictator — by definition — is the most complete collectivist of all, because he exists by ruling, crushing and exploiting a huge collective of men.

Don't permit the snide little touches which Communists sneak into scripts — all the lines, hints and implications which suggest that something (a person, an attitude, a motive, an emotion) is evil because it is independent (or private, or personal, or single, or individual).

Don't preach that everything done for others is good, while everything done for one's own sake is evil. This damns every form of personal joy and happiness.

Don't preach that everything "public-spirited" is good, while everything personal and private is evil.

Don't make every form of loneliness a sin, and every form of the herd spirit a virtue.

Remember that America is the country of the pioneer, the non-conformist, the inventor, the originator, the innovator. Remember that all the great thinkers, artists, scientists were single, individual, independent men who stood alone, and discovered new directions of achievement — alone.

Don't let yourself be fooled when the Reds tell you that what they want to destroy are men like Hitler or Mussolini. What they want to destroy are men like Shakespeare, Chopin and Edison.

If you doubt this, think of a certain movie, in which a great composer was damned for succumbing, temporarily, to a horrible, vicious, selfish, anti-social sin. What was his sin? That he wanted to sit alone in his room and write music!

12. Don't Use Current Events Carelessly.

A favorite trick of the Communists is to insert into pictures casual lines of dialogue about some important, highly controversial political issue, to insert them as accidental small talk, without any connection to the scene, the plot, or the story.

Don't permit such lines. **Don't** permit snide little slurs at any political party — in a picture which is to be released just before election time.

Don't allow chance remarks of a partisan nature about any current political events.

If you wish to mention politics on the screen, or take sides in a current controversy — then do so fully and openly. Even those who do not agree with you will respect an honest presentation of the side you've chosen. But the seemingly accidental remarks, the casual wisecracks, the cowardly little half-hints are the things that arouse the anger and contempt of all those who uphold the opposite side of the issue. In most of the current issues, that opposite side represents half or more than half of your picture audience.

And it is a sad joke on Hollywood that while we shy away from all controversial subjects on the screen, in order not to antagonize anybody — we arouse more antagonism throughout the country and more resentment against ourselves by one cheap little smear line in the midst of some musical comedy than we ever would by a whole political treatise.

Of all current questions, be most careful about your attitude toward Soviet Russia. You do not have to make pro-Soviet or anti-Soviet pictures, if you do not wish to take a stand. But if you claim that you wish to remain neutral, **don't** stick into pictures casual lines favorable to Soviet Russia. Look out for remarks that praise Russia directly or indirectly; or statements to the effect that anyone who is anti-Soviet is pro-Fascist; or references to fictitious Soviet achievements.

Don't suggest to the audience that the Russian people are free, secure and happy, that life in Russia is just about the same as in any other country — while actually the Russian people live in constant terror under a bloody, monstrous dictatorship. Look out for speeches that support whatever is in the Soviet interests of the moment, whatever is part of the current Communist party line. **Don't** permit dialogue such as: "The free, peace-loving nations of the world —

America, England, and Russia ..." or, "Free elections, such as in Poland ..." or, "American imperialists ought to get out of China ..."

13. Don't Smear American Political Institutions.

The Communist Party Line takes many turns and makes many changes to meet shifting conditions. But on one objective it has remained fixed: to undermine faith in and ultimately to destroy our American political institutions.

Don't discredit the Congress of the United States by presenting it as an ineffectual body, devoted to mere talk. If you do that — you imply that representative government is no good, and what we ought to have is a dictator.

Don't discredit our free elections. If you do that — you imply that elections should be abolished.

Don't discredit our courts by presenting them as corrupt. If you do that — you lead people to believe that they have no recourse except to violence, since peaceful justice cannot be obtained.

It is true that there have been vicious Congressmen and judges, and politicians who have stolen elections, just as there are vicious men in any profession. But if you present them in a story, be sure to make it clear that you are criticizing particular men — **not the system**. The American system, as such, is the best ever devised in history. If some men do not live up to it — let us damn these men, **not** the system which they betray.

Conclusion

These are the things which Communists and their sympathizers try to sneak into pictures intended as non-political — and these are the things which you must keep out of your scripts, if your intention is to make non-political movies.

There is, of course, no reason why you should not make pictures on political themes. In fact, it would be most desirable if there were more pictures advocating the political principles of Americanism, seriously, consistently and dramatically. Serious themes are always good entertainment, if honestly done. But if you attempt such pictures — do not undertake them lightly, carelessly, and with no better equipment than a few trite generalities and safe, benevolent bromides. Be very sure of what you want to say — and say it clearly, specifically, uncompromisingly. Evasions and generalities only help the enemies of Americanism — by giving people the impression that American principles are a collection of weak, inconsistent, meaningless, hypocritical, worn-out old slogans.

There is no obligation on you to make political pictures — if you do not wish to take a strong stand. You are free to confine your work to good, honest, non-political movies. But **there is** a moral obligation on you to present the political ideas of Americanism strongly and honestly — if you undertake pictures with political themes.

And when you make pictures with political themes and implications — **DON'T** hire Communists to write, direct or produce them. You cannot expect Communists to remain "neutral" and not to insert their own ideas into their work. Take them at **their** word, not ours. **They** have declared openly and repeatedly that their first obligation is to the Communist Party, that their first duty is to spread Party propaganda, and that their work in pictures is only a means to an end, the end being the Dictatorship of the Proletariat. You had better believe them about their own stated intentions. Remember that Hitler, too, stated openly that his aim was world conquest, but nobody believed him or took him seriously until it was too late.

Now a word of warning about the question of free speech. The principle of free speech requires that we do not use **police force** to forbid the Communists the expression of their ideas — which means that we do not **pass laws** forbidding them to speak. But the principle of free speech **does not** require that we furnish the Communists with the means to preach their ideas, and **does not** imply that we owe them jobs and support to advocate our own destruction at our own expense. The Constitutional guaranty of free speech reads: "Congress shall pass no law . . ." It does not require employers to be suckers.

Let the Communists preach what they wish (so long as it remains mere talking) at the expense of those and in the employ of those who share their ideas. Let them create their own motion picture studios, if they can. But let us put an end to their use of our pictures, our studios and our money for the purpose of preaching our expropriation, enslavement and destruction. Freedom of speech does not imply that it is our duty to provide a knife for the murderer who wants to cut our throat.

Motion Picture Alliance for the Preservation of American Ideals

Statement of Principles

We believe in, and like, the American way of life: the liberty and freedom which generations before us have fought to create and preserve; the freedom to speak, to think, to live, to worship, to work, and to govern ourselves as individuals, as free men; the right to succeed or fail as free men, according to the measure of our ability and our strength.

Believing in these things, we find ourselves in sharp revolt against a rising tide of communism, fascism, and kindred beliefs, that seek by subversive means to undermine and change this way of life; groups that have forfeited their right to exist in this country of ours, because they seek to achieve their change by means other than the vested procedure of the ballot and to deny the right of the majority opinion of the people to rule.

In our special field of motion pictures, we resent the growing impression that this industry is made of, and dominated by, Communists, radicals, and crackpots. We believe that we represent the vast majority of the people who serve this great medium of expression. But unfortunately it has been an unorganized majority. This has been almost inevitable. The very love of freedom, of the rights of the individual, make this great majority reluctant to organize. But now we must, or we shall meanly lose "the last, best hope on earth."

As Americans, we have no new plan to offer. We want no new plan, we want only to defend against its enemies that which is our priceless heritage; that freedom which has given man, in this country, the fullest life and the richest expression the world has ever known; that system which, in the present emergency, has fathered an effort that, more than any other single factor, will make possible the winning of this war.

As members of the motion-picture industry, we must face and accept an especial responsibility. Motion pictures are inescapably one of the world's greatest forces for influencing public thought and opinion, both at home and abroad. In this fact lies solemn obligation. We refuse to permit the effort of Communist, Fascist, and other totalitarian-minded groups to pervert this powerful medium into an instrument for the dissemination of un-American ideas and beliefs. We pledge ourselves to fight, with every means at our organized command, any effort of any group or individual, to divert the loyalty of the screen from the free America that give it birth. And to dedicate our work, in the fullest possible measure, to the presentation of the American scene, its standards and its freedoms, its beliefs and its ideals, as we know them and believe in them.

Other books in this Time Capsule Collection are available and/or forthcoming. For more Visit: OffBeatReads.com

www.ingramcontent.com/pod-product-compliance
Lightning Source LLC
Chambersburg PA
CBHW030202100526
44592CB00009B/409